Broken Bits & Pieces

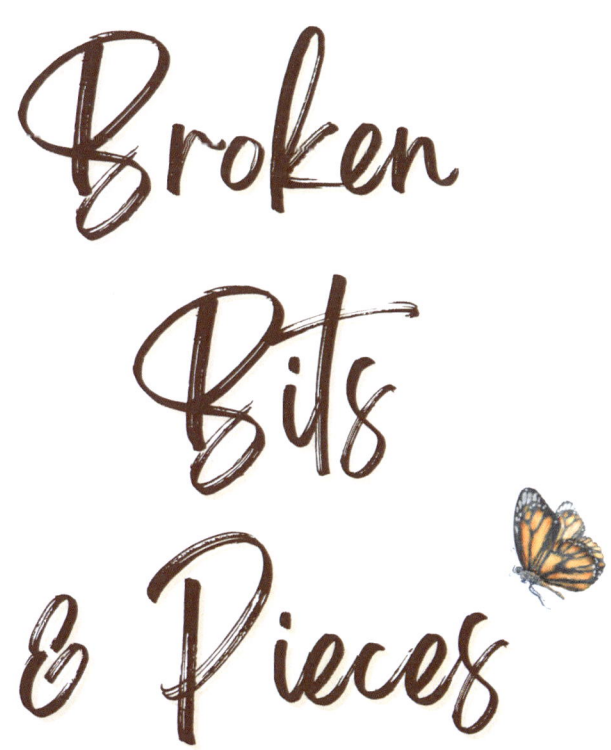

A JOURNEY THROUGH POETRY AND SELF-DISCOVERY

CARLA SAMMS

Dedicated to:

Janice Kerr
Stephanie Layne
Jason Samms
Avion Smith- Samms
Michelle Robinson Powell

BROKEN BITS & PIECES

ISBN:
Hardcover: 978-1-998245-35-2
Paperback: 978-1-998245-34-5

Cover and book design by Kabrena L. Robinson
Published by Eva-Michelle & Family Publishing
www.evamichelleandfamily.com

Contents

Introduction

Welcome to **Broken Bits & Pieces**, a poetry and guided journal designed to support your journey of self-discovery and healing. This book offers more than words on a page—it is a space for reflection, expression, and growth.

Life's challenges often leave us with broken fragments—moments of pain, doubt, and uncertainty. In these pages, you will explore those pieces and begin to weave them into something whole. Each section focuses on a stage of healing: acknowledging pain, embracing identity, finding strength, navigating the healing journey, and moving forward with hope.

The poetry within each section touches on universal themes of resilience and empowerment. Following each poem, you will find prompts and journaling activities to guide your reflection and encourage self-expression. These are designed to help you connect with your story and explore the emotions these poems evoke.

You are invited to use this book in your own way. Take your time with each section, revisit pages as needed, and allow yourself to feel deeply. My hope is that you will see yourself in these pages, find strength in your story, and leave this journey feeling whole and empowered.

Let us begin together.

Author's Note

I wrote this poetry book to share my story and experiences—the challenges I have faced and how I overcame them. Let this book be your safe space to release all your feelings and emotions.

I want you to know that even though you may feel alone, you are not. You might feel like no one can relate to you, but others can and may even be going through worse. You might be afraid or feel like you cannot express yourself, fearing that no one will understand or that you will be misunderstood. You may feel like no one cares, but I do.

I hope this book gives you confidence and encourages you to hold on and not give up because you have a purpose—we all have a purpose. Your time to rise and overcome may seem far away, but hold on. In the end, you will have your own story to tell, one that speaks of your life's journey.

With gratitude and encouragement,

Carla Samms

Learn More:
www.Carlasamms.com

Acknowledging Pain

These poems focus on the pain of isolation,
confusion, and emotional wounds.

The Black Sheep

Family members gather together,
Laugh, chat, and eat.
Where am I?
I am there. (but not with them) I am isolated–
The black sheep.
Why am I not with my family?
I can't.
Same building, but it feels like we are worlds apart.
It wouldn't feel right.
It would be awkward,
Like I am intruding.
We are related by blood, but
I am not one of them.
I am different.
I am special.
I am the black sheep.
I am not upset;
I am hurt.
There is no communication,
No equality.
Who am I to complain?
I'm just the black sheep.
When I make it,
Will they regret it,
How they treated this black sheep?

If I did, I would only be bombarded with questions.
They don't reach out, but
When they do it's only to know my plans.
Who am I to complain?
I'm just the black sheep.

Help

I need help.
I feel lost and confused.
My mind feels as if it is overheating.
There are too many issues,
Too many words that I want to say,
But instead, they are bottled up and left unsaid.
Too much pressure
From myself.
I made myself a disappointment.
I am the worthless one.
All along it hasn't been said,
But I can see that now.
I've always noticed that I'm compared with someone.
I'm always told that I have it easy.
Not because I look physically stable,
It doesn't mean my mind is too.
You can't see how much I beat myself up
Because there are no marks.
You don't see how much I blame myself
Because there is no proof.
The amount of time I question why I was born–
Because I don't know my purpose.
I haven't found it yet.
Right now, all I am doing is causing pain.

It doesn't make any sense for me to speak or explain,
Because what would come out of my mouth
Would just be received as "excuses".
I need help.

What's Next?

You call me names.
You say all I do is tell lies.
You put all the blame on me;
You are never in the wrong.
What's next?
Will it ever end,
Or will you keep blaming me?
Your words feel as if a knife is piercing through my skin.
How does it feel
To do the pointing, casting stones?
What's next?
You compare me to others;
It's as if I am useless.
To you, I never make an effort;
To you, my efforts are never enough.
What's next?
Anything that involves me is not worth mentioning;
Anything that has to do with me is never good for you.
I could make the headlines, and you still wouldn't
acknowledge me.
You are too focused on everyone and everything else
That you forget entirely about me.
What's next?
What about me? Am I not also one of your own?

You make me feel as if I am a stranger
In the one place I can call my home.
Am I not a person who deserves the same love you give to
the others?

Self Reflection

What experiences have shaped my understanding of pain?

Self
Reflection

How do I cope with my emotions?

Journal

Use this space to write about your feelings and describe moments when you felt lost or overwhelmed. Feel free to let it all out.

Embracing Identity

These poems explore self-expression and coming to terms with one's unique identity.

Express Yourself

Express yourself,
Tell them how you feel.
If you cannot say it, write it.
What is on your mind?
Since no one can see inside or read your mind, draw it.
If they don't understand,
At least you can say you tried
To express yourself.
Express yourself,
Don't be a slave to your thoughts or emotions.
To move on, you've got to express yourself.
What will you gain from holding it in?
Pain, hate and suffering.
What will you gain from letting go?
FREEDOM.
With freedom comes
Growth, opportunities, making new connections,
and starting new chapters.
Express yourself.
What will you lose?
Will your loss be more than your gain
If you express yourself?

This is my advice to me and you.

Be Real

Be real.
You play the role of being perfect,
then go on to say you are human.
You point the blame at someone
who has been there from the beginning.
You speak in a soft tone to draw me in,
so I let down my guard and tell you what my next move is.
You try to get in my head to know what I am thinking.
You use code whenever you speak.
Don't try to undermine my intelligence.
Stop using code when you are speaking.
I am not a fool.
I take this as a sign that I am no longer needed.
Now, when I am leaving,
you are giving me compliments more than you did before.
There is a saying: the cow doesn't know
the use of its tail until it is gone.
Now that is the case.
It is my time to move on.

Part 1: You Don't Know Me

You don't know my story, though.

And *you* don't know my song.

You don't know how I lived and what's going on.

You have your own story, though it may be rough.

My life was and still is tough.

You only see the pieces, but *you* don't know the picture.

Though *you* have an image painted,

What is my story actually saying?

You only speak, but that is it.

But if *you're* the only one talking, is that really communicating?

You state your demands and expectations, but that is it–*you're* not listening.

You point out my flaws as if I need fixing.

Am I a robot that is malfunctioning?

The last time I checked, I was a human with feelings.

Now that my decision is made,

Thanks to *you*, now I'll change.

Self
Reflection

What makes me unique?

Self Reflection

In what ways have I felt misunderstood?

Exercise

Create Your Personal Identity Manifesto

This exercise will help you to embrace your identity by defining your core values and beliefs, leading to the creation of a personal manifesto.

Step 1: List Your Core Values

Write down values that guide your life. These are principles you hold important, such as integrity, kindness, courage, or authenticity.

....

....

....

Step 2: Identify Key Beliefs

Reflect on your beliefs about yourself and the world.

Consider:
- What do I believe about my worth and purpose?
- How do I view challenges in life?

....

....

....

....

....

....

....

....

....

....

Step 3: Write Your Manifesto

Use your values and beliefs to craft a short, empowering statement about who you are and how you choose to live.

....

....

....

....

....

....

Step 4: Affirm Daily

Revisit your manifesto regularly to remind yourself of your guiding principles and stay aligned with them.

Finding
Strength

These poems reflect personal empowerment and the courage to stand up for oneself.

Push And Pull

When I say I don't want to talk about it,
It means give me time.
When I say I want to be by myself,
don't push or start questioning me.
I am not your child.
I have my own mind, and I can make my own decisions.
I will listen to your suggestions, but at the end of the day,
it is still up to me.
Whether or not I choose to take it.
Who do you see me as?
As someone who will continue to let you push her buttons?
Once a button is spoiled, there is no turning back.
It is about time for me to take a stand (up).
When a cup is full,
As long as the water is running, it will run over.
Am I a fool to let you keep rubbing salt in my wounds?
Are you that blind you cannot see the ones you are hurting?
Your flesh is so thick that even if the truth came flying your way,
you wouldn't feel it.
I am not a prey, but push a prey for too long, it'll turn on you.
When I'm trying to move on, you find every way to make this a
cycle.

How am I supposed to grow when you keep pushing me down?

I need fresh ground and fresh soil.

I don't belong here anymore.

It is time for me to be like an eagle—be free and one with the wind.

It is time for me to level up and see the full view of what's waiting for me.

It's Your Time

When was the last time you checked in with you?
When was the last time you treated yourself?
When was the last time the main focus was you?
When was the last time you placed yourself first?
If you had to think about it,
That means it is time.
It is your time.
Time to look after you.
Time to prioritize your needs.
Time to give yourself a break.
Time to give yourself the attention you need.
Time to appreciate you.
Time to get your thoughts together.
Time to get organized.
You owe that time to yourself.
Time for self-love.
It is your time.

Part 2: You Don't Know Me (You Don't Own Me)

I will no longer respond
When you throw questions at me.
I am not a suspect or criminal of a crime,
To be pushed into a corner and be interrogated.
I have the right to remain silent.
When I choose and decide to speak,
You should not be offended.
You should not say I have no respect.
Time after time, you voiced your feelings;
I sat and listened–that is the difference.
When I speak, it is as if my words are insignificant.
This time it is over; I will no longer give time to where I am no
longer needed.
Now it is my time to heal,
My time to vent,
My time to move on and focus on myself.
Time waits for no one.
Once it is gone, you can never get it back.
I no longer want to live life with regrets.
I want to go forward and refind myself,
The me that was free and had some confidence,
Not the me now who feels like I've got nothing left.

Self Reflection

How does this poems resonate with you?

Self Reflection

What are some strengths you have discovered in yourself that you didn't know you had?

Exercise

Finding Strength Through Gratitude and Reflection

Gratitude List

Write down 3 things you are grateful for today. These can be small or big—anything that brings you a sense of appreciation.

1. ....

2. ....

3. ....

Personal Victories

Reflect on and list 2 moments where you showed courage or overcame a challenge, no matter how small.

1. ....

2. ....

Affirmations

Write down some affirmations that remind you of your strength. These should be empowering statements that help boost your confidence.

Revisit these lists when you need encouragement or strength.

....

....

....

....

....

....

....

....

....

The Healing Journey

These poems speak to the process of
healing from past hurts and the struggle to
keep going.

Close To The Edge

I am hurt, I am broken.
But how would anyone know?
I smile, and I laugh—"Everything is alright,"
I say to myself and everyone else.
But I am close to the edge,
My mind, my broken heart.
The pain I feel, I keep it to myself,
Afraid no one would understand,
Mainly because I have been mostly misunderstood,
Leaving me close to the edge.
I try my best to not look over my shoulder
Because of the fear—
My mind is overtaken by my fear
Of no one being there when I turn around.
I am close to the edge.
I keep a positive face because that's what everyone is used to
seeing.
Now I am not so sure if I can keep it up much longer.
I am close to the edge.
I want someone to notice
That I am struggling to hold on.
That I am weak and don't have much energy left,
To pull me back so I am no longer close to the edge.

Road With Many Holes

The sight of everyone moving forward
When you have just begun your journey can be very difficult.
I know because it is something I have also experienced myself.
It makes you rethink the decisions you have made,
If the path you took was the right way,
If you should start over again or keep going.
To give up because you fell into so many holes,
Not sure if you can get up again.
The ones you love,
The ones you look forward to for encouragement
when you fall,
Are long gone ahead,
Nowhere in sight.
You wonder when it will be your time–
Your time to shine,
Your time to experience success,
Your time to see the harvest of your hard work.
You start to second-guess your potential.
If you'll ever make it out of the hole.
Though you started your journey at the same time,
You can see that the distance is very apparent.
You start to think if you should pick up the pace
you are going,

So that you can " fit in".
While you're trying to figure out what works best for you
They already began getting ready to start their new journey,
Leaving you on a lonely road with many holes.

Pain

Pain is not meant to be endured,
Nor does it mean you should give up.
You should take action;
Do not settle.
Do something about it
For your own good.
You deserve more than this—
More than what you are going through.
Know when to set a boundary;
Know when to stop putting others' well-being before yours.
Pain can't be avoided but can be learned from.
Acknowledge that you are in pain;
Identify the cause of that pain.
Take the lessons from it,
Make a change in your life,
And move on.

Self Reflection

When have I felt the strongest?

Self Reflection

How can I practice self-compassion?

Exercise

Healing Through Visualization and Creative Expression

Guided Visualization

Close your eyes and imagine a place where you feel completely safe and at peace. This could be a real or imagined space. Once you've created this space in your mind, write down your experience:

- What does this safe place look like?

....

....

....

- How do you feel when you are there?

....

....

....

- Who, if anyone, is with you?

....

....

....

Artistic Expression

Use this space to draw or sketch what your healing journey looks like to you. It could be abstract— colors, shapes, or patterns—or a literal representation of your growth. Let your creativity flow without judgment.

Moving Forward

Self Reflection

What does letting go mean to you?

Self Reflection

Who are you becoming as you heal?

Creative Writing Prompt

Write a short letter to yourself from your future self
—someone who has healed and grown through the
challenges you're facing now. What advice, comfort,
or encouragement would they offer?

Notes

A safe space for you to express more

www.ingramcontent.com/pod-product-compliance
Lightning Source LLC
Chambersburg PA
CBRC090835120626
46547CB00011B/695